GIR

CW00497872

by Sarah Richardson

‖SAMUEL FRENCH‖

FOR PRODUCTION ENQUIRIES

UNITED KINGDOM AND WORLD
EXCLUDING NORTH AMERICA
licensing@concordtheatricals.co.uk

020-7054-7298

NORTH AMERICA
info@concordtheatricals.com
1-866-979-0447

Each title is subject to availability from Concord Theatricals,
depending upon country of performance.

GIRLPLAY was first performed at theSpace on North bridge for the Edinburgh Festival on 5th August 2022. Produced by Sarah Richardson with SJ Woods. The cast was as follows:

A . . . . .Sarah Richardson
B . . . . Laura Brady
C . . . . .Martha Dunlea

CAST

SARAH RICHARDSON | "A" (Playwright/Co-Producer)
Sarah Richardson is an actor, playwright and spoken word poet. She trained at the Gaiety School of Acting in Ireland and appeared in a number of the Gaiety's Shakespeare productions including *Macbeth* and *King Lear*. Alongside *GirlPlay*, Sarah has appeared in other self-penned work such as *A Ton Of Feathers* that was presented at the NSDF festival 2022 as part of the NSDF Lab programme and was the recipient of the Axis Assemble Associate Artist programme (2020) and FringeLab Artist programme (2020) for her work on her one woman show *Sun Bear*.

LAURA BRADY | "B"
Theatre includes: *The Roaring Banshees* (Smock Alley Theatre); *TINS* (The Boys School); *How Far, Antigone?* (Teatrelabor, Bielefeld); *Flaming Inspirations* (Samuel Beckett Theatre); *Essex Birds* (Smock Alley Theatre); *Triangles* (The International Comedy Club) and *Romeo and Juliet* (The Samuel Beckett Theatre). Film includes: *Soft Places* (Independent); *Crone Wood* (Blacklodge Films); *Proclaim!* (Three Hot Whiskies Production).

MARTHA DUNLEA | "C"
Martha is an Irish actor living in London. She graduated from the MA Acting for Screen course at The Royal Central School of Speech and Drama in 2021. She most recently worked on the world premiere of *Baile Beag Mór*, written and directed by IFTA nominated filmmaker Philip Doherty with Fibín sa Taibhdhearc. Other recent credits include: *GirlPlay* at Camden People's Theatre and Dublin Fringe Festival; *Eclipsed* at The Mill Dundrum; *Macbeth* with Fibín, *Dancing at Lughnasa* at The Everyman Cork and *The Shaughraun* at Smock Alley Theatre Dublin.
Martha recently worked with BAFTA winning director David Blaire on *The Reckoning* for ITV, which aired in 2022.

CREATIVE TEAM

CIARA ELIZABETH SMYTH | Director
Ciara Elizabeth Smyth is an Irish writer and director for stage and screen. Her plays have been presented by the Abbey Theatre, Fishamble, Dublin Fringe Festival, the MAC Theatre, Project Arts Centre and Bewley's Café Theatre. She currently has several new projects in development for TV, including adaptations of her debut play, *All honey*, (Fishamble New Writing Award 2017) and her 2019 play *SAUCE*. Ciara is a recipient of the Next Generation Award 2020, the Lyric Theatre's Live to Digital Commission 2021, the Abbey Theatre's Commemoration Bursary 2021 and was accepted to Sharp Shorts 2022, a development fund to create her first short film. Ciara is represented by Nick Marston and Katie Battcock in Curtis Brown.

SJ WOODS | Creative Producer/Assistant Director
SJ Woods is a London-based Creative Producer from the West of Ireland. She makes immersive and multi-sensory theatre experiences inspired by place, identity, class and the visceral subject matter that this provides. Her work has an international focus and cross pollinates between theatre, live art and film, often pushing conventional theatrical boundaries to off-site locations.

SJ came on board as Creative Producer of *GirlPlay* in Spring 2021 bringing it to Camden People's Theatre later that year and to Edinburgh Fringe in 2022.

JENNIFER O'MALLEY | Sound Designer
Jennifer is a composer and sound designer based in Dublin who is a classically trained multi-instrumentalist and vocalist. She primarily composes electronic and orchestral music, often blending the two using her cello (among other acoustic instruments) and synthesisers while her sound design explores moving from organic to non-diegetic sound worlds.
Some of her theatre credits as a composer & sound designer include: *Summertime* (Dublin Fringe, 2018, Drogheda Arts Festival, 2019, Abbey Young Curators Festival, 2019); *Iphigenia In Splott* (Smock Alley Theatre, 2018); *We Can't Have Monkeys In The House* (Peacock Theatre, 2019); *SAUCE* (Bewley's Cafe Theatre, 2019); *Restoration* (Project Arts Centre, 2020); *Venus In Fur* (Project Arts Centre, 2020); *SHIT* (Project Arts Centre, 2020); *Will I See You There* (Dublin Fringe, 2020); *Before You Say Anything* (Dublin Fringe, 2020); *Ar Ais Arís* (Brightening Air, 2021); *Goodnight Egg* (Civic Theatre, 2021); *Where Sat the Lovers* (Dublin Fringe, 2021); *Masterclass* (Dublin Fringe, 2021); *You're Still Here* (Dublin Fringe, 2021); *Absent The Wrong* (Dublin Fringe Festival, 2022); *Good Sex* (Dublin Theatre Festival, 2022). www.jenny.ie

AMY DANIELS | Lighting Designer

Amy (she/her) is a London-based freelance lighting designer, production manager and technician. A lover of theatre since she can remember, she studied English Literature at the University of Sussex and fell in love with production during a year abroad at SUNY Stony Brook. She is the Technical Manager at Camden People's Theatre and designs for a wide variety of performances. Find her full credits and portfolio on her website - www.amydanielslighting.com.

ÁINE O'HARA | Set, Costume and Graphic Designer

Áine O'Hara is a Dublin based multidisciplinary artist, theatre maker and designer. They are interested in creating work that blurs the lines between community building and art. Áine has presented work nationally and internationally and their work has been supported by Dublin Fringe Festival, A4 sounds studios, Arts and Disability Ireland and the Arts Council of Ireland. You can see more about their work at aineohara.com

Established in 1995, theSpaceUK specialise in producing live performance. Our theatres have become widely recognised as the home of award-winning theatre and new work at the Edinburgh Festival Fringe. We host the largest and most diverse programme at the Festival, offering an array of new writing, theatre, dance, music, children's and family shows, comedy, drama, sketch, cabaret, opera, a capella, exhibitions, events and stand-up comedy shows. Our passion is relentless and our expertise extensive as we offer the Festival's most progressive and original platform.

"Where gems emerge." – *The Scotsman*

When the 2020 pandemic hit, theSpaceUK launched Online@ theSpaceUK to allow companies and artists from all over the world to take part in the largest virtual festival in the world. *GirlPlay* was the star of Online@theSpaceUK Season 2, picking up awards, rave reviews and global audience acclaim. A courageous cast and production team meant that GirlPlay was a powerful and emotive show that richly deserved these plaudits.

"theSpaceUK has the kind of lovely, unheralded work that will surprise audiences once more onEdinburgh stages." – *The Stage*

theSpaceUK champions new work and new artists. As part of this support theSpaceUK offers a Supported Artists Programme to new and innovative work, providing financial, marketing and production support. We are delighted to announce that *GirlPlay*, written by Sarah Richardson, is one of the Supported Artists for 2022.

CHARACTERS

A

B

C

AUTHOR'S NOTES

I started writing *GirlPlay* in 2018/19. I had been writing and performing poetry for a few years at this point and a lot of my work already focused on sex and relationships, however I wanted to write something bigger. When it came to sex, there was so much more I wanted to explore that I could never fully fit a three-minute poem. There were so many situations, moments and dynamics that I wanted the space and the scope to examine more deeply. So, with the original poems creating a basis for the play, *GirlPlay* was born.

GirlPlay has had a journey to get to this point, as most shows created right before the pandemic have. From a work in progress showing at Scene and Heard and debuting at Dublin Fringe 2019 to being turned into an audio play and touring internationally online, winning Best Digital Experience at Stockholm Fringe 2020. It was restaged at the end of 2021 for a three-night run at Camden People's Theatre in preparation for Edinburgh Fringe 2022. All of this is to say that sometimes it has been a bit of a mission and there have been obstacles along the way, but I am really pleased that as a team we have been able to keep *GirlPlay* alive over the last few years and get it to where we are today.

When writing *GirlPlay* I wanted it to be a piece that could discuss sex and women's sexual experience honestly. I wanted it to be awkward and funny and pleasurable and sexy and heart-breaking and painful all at once. Sex is never one thing. What it is to me, will be different from what it is to you. But my hope is that there will be at least one moment in the play that will make you feel seen and understood or that it will help you to see and understand others.

I don't really know why so much of my work focuses around sex, I think it has led to people believing that I am obsessed with the subject (and I'm not saying I'm not obsessed, I think a good portion of people are) I just find it interesting that something that is so heavily present in our society, amongst our peers and in our culture can still be laced with so much taboo and stigma. Sex is everywhere, constantly, yet for a lot of people and a lot of communities sexual expression and sexual pleasure is still not a conversation that can be had freely. I'm almost annoyed that a play like this is even still relevant, but here we are. As a woman, I wanted to create a piece that depicted the many complexities, good and bad, that we encounter in relationships when it comes to sex. And I wanted to go beyond just the sex itself. There is so much shame when it comes to women having sex and enjoying sex and wanting sex. There is so much shame around women and their bodies. There is so much shame around motherhood and pregnancies and miscarriages. And shame leads to silence. Silence in pleasure. Silence in pain. Silence in our experiences. I hope that, even in a small way, this play can break down some of those silences.

Finally I want to thank everyone who has supported or been involved with *GirlPlay* so far. It is fair to say this play wouldn't have happened without all the generosity and support it has been offered personally and professionally. Thanks to my amazing creative team, Scene and Heard, Dublin Fringe, Fishamble, theSpaceUK, Concord. And, last but not least, a massive thank you to my family, whose unwavering support, advice and encouragement is a constant that I can always rely on.

NOTES ON STAGING

A, B and C are all the same character.

"..." - indicates when a character is trailing off or avoiding saying a word

"/" - indicates lines being cut off/short or when characters are finishing sentences/talking over each other in conversation

"-" - indicates lines being interrupted or when characters lines are in their own moments rather than conversation

For Mum, Dad and James,
Thank you for everything.

A. I sit here

B. Look at me

A. Sitting here

C. Cramped in

A. Sitting here

B. Wet

C. Cramped in

A. Sitting here

C. Looking at me

A. I sit here

B. Too late

C. Is it too late?

A. To sit here

B. And start

A. I want them

B. Their millions of nerves

C. Their heartbeat

B. Something with a heartbeat

A. I want

C. A beat

A. I want

B. Them

C. To sit here

B. With me

A. And

B. It hurts

C. It's suffocating

B. It's isolating

C. But it's funny

A. I could

C. Laugh

A. Because it's funny

B. Me

A. Sitting here

B. You

C. Looking at me

A. Sitting here

C. Look

B. At

A. Me

B. I want

C. You

B. Let me help

C. You heal

A. My body can heal

C. Heal my body

B. We can heal

A. Trace

B. Trace my skin

C. Connecting

B. Everything

A. Connecting every inch

C. Inch closer

B. And now you

C. Look

B. At

A. Me

C. As I

A. Sit here

B. Sparkling

C. It's sparkling

B. I'm looking like

C. I want

A. My

B. I want

A. Me

C. I want

A. No?

B. Maybe

C. Yes

A. I want to

B. Try

C. To pump life

B. To consume

C. To play

A. To sit here

B. And look at me

C. I want

A. To sit here

C. And start

A. To try

B. A touch

A. To try

C. Touching

A. Me

B. I want to

A. Sit here

C. Cramped in

B. Wet

A. I want to sit here

C. And

B. Understand

A. I want you

B. I want them

C. I want me

A. So I

B. Touch

A. And I start

      (Beat.)

   Seven

C. I don't know when I first became aware of it.

B. I thought it was something that just held my wee,

A. And then suddenly, it's sparkling

C. Sort of tingling

B. Like it's giggling.

A. It's funny

B. A funny feeling.

C. Something's happening.

B. Beyond my understanding.

A. And then I'm standing,

C. Looking in a mirror

B. Looking at me.

A. And looking back at me

C. I'm wondering?

A. What's that funny thing?

> *(Beat.)*

B. And then later, I'm in the bath,

A. Sitting in Mum's used water,

C. And I don't know why but I'm bashing barbies together.

A. Smashing their bodies, on top of each other

C. Legs split open, aggressively hitting them against one another.

B. Rubbing their smooth areas up and down and around the others,

C. And it's funny,

A. Because there's that feeling,

B. That sparkling,

A. But nothing's happening,

B. The barbies are just sort of slipping.

C. And I'm wondering?

A. Where are their funny things?

> *(Beat.)*

C. Eighteen

B. And I don't know when it transitioned from being that funny thing that I peed out of to being something else.

C. Something exciting, something bad, something...

A. I remember the first time I touched it, like properly investigated it.

C. It was like when you are doing a word search and you've got one word left to find and you've been staring at the page for so long that you actually start to think there is a mistake, like maybe they forgot to put that word in there or something. And so you start compiling a letter of complaint in your head, when you see it. And it's now as if that word is in bold letters and every time you look at the page it's all you can see. It was like that.

A. I was in the shower.

C. And for girls it's really hard to masturbate standing up, but it's not like anyone told me that or gave me a wanking masterclass, so I just had to sort of work it out for myself. I tried opening my legs as wide as possible and got a sort of squat on.

B. But my thighs gave way so I tried rubbing away, one leg up against the wall, bent over, water running down my face, hair sticking to my cheeks, blurred vision.

A. Luckily we had one of those shower/bath combos.

B. So there I was, back in our family bath only this time I'm cramped in, legs open as wide as the sides would go, elbows hitting the support handles, shower pounding down on me, the water cold by the time it had left the shower head and hit my body and then/

ALL. Boom.

(Pause.)

B. I thought I had peed myself.

I found that button and my whole body spasmed, feet kicking taps, head smacking into shampoo bottles, Mum calling to ask if I was alright.

ALL. Yeah, fine thanks, just stubbed my toe.

A. What the... just happened?

B. Is that normal?

C. Should I have done that?

B. After the first time I couldn't stop.

C. I couldn't believe anyone stopped. Ever.

A. I heard of a woman who can have an orgasm just from thinking, in like two minutes. How the hell does she get anything done? I wouldn't. I wouldn't be able to focus.

C. It would be like the best superpower ever...

B. And the worst,

C. Because how would I fight crime? I would be too busy getting myself off.

B. I couldn't understand why no-one talked about this. Why no-one mentioned it before? Why other girls didn't do it.

A. I mean, women wouldn't have been given clits if they weren't meant to be enjoyed.

ALL. Right?

(Beat.)

C. Twenty one

B. Sure, I was a late bloomer

C. And everyone else came sooner

B. And I was one of the fewer

A. But we few had each other. And this was a big night, my night.

My 21st

So we went out.

Like out out

Out of our family homes

Down the road

Turn right onto the high street

And there it was.

ALL. The Club

C. Of course we knew it, but we hadn't actually been to it,

Everyone in the town knew it,

We were just new to it.

To this

To being out

To being out out

It wasn't really our thing

But tonight it was happening.

We walked in,

The smell of sweat was shocking

It had eroded the walls till they were dripping, the paper curling at its edges

We edged in further

Uncomfortably squirming in our overdressed dresses

Tripping over abandoned heels, abandoned bags, abandoned lads.

What am I doing here?

B. We make a beeline for the bar,

And people slip and drinks tip as we fight to get served.

And in the exchange of money for drinks I struggle to hear what the barman's saying over the thud of a beat bashing in my head

What am I doing here?

A. I lean in,

I put my hands on the bar to push myself up to hear and they stick,

Becoming attached so I have to physically unpeel them from stickiness that clings to them.

From what I hope is just alcohol and not a mix of the saliva dripping from the open mouth, of the tongue licking olympic team, going for gold next to me.

What am I doing here?

I don't belong here

I go to move

Maybe to leave/

C. And then *You* walk in, talking, girls trip and fall in at your feet.

You never miss a beat as you meet and greet your fans. You stand, tall but cool, happy to take a back seat as people taxi along with you, I'm with you.

And for a second I catch your eye and I think,

Fuck

What if he was mine?

B. But see I'm not a massively sexually experienced person.

From Barbies to bathtubs, I haven't quite graduated to full on sex stuff.

Sure I have kissed and maybe once or twice a hand might have slipped but the opportunity for anything else was just sort of missed.

Shocked? I know right but look at me; –

Lacking class, tight ass, big ask to take me: a geeky Dr Who fan, who can't stick it to the man and doesn't really have any plan at all.

And least of all, this exposed, protruding nose, sticky out chin and a brace for a grin.

And I know that my mum teaches me that it's these quirky features in me that make me stand out... right out of that line of another kind of fucking fit ass girls.

I mean, Jesus Christ, that's some good DNA.

But it's okay because Mum says that's what makes me unconventionally beautiful.

C. But right now I don't want unconventional I want Your attention so I fall into every stereotypical intention;

As I clench in, wrenched in, end up drenched in anything to fit into perfection.

Beauty's pain as I get slain by the blisters forming as I conform into wearing these lace up, waist up, trying to keep my face up boots.

B. Because really, I wish I could be in that line of fit ass girls.

In the club with their arses hypnotising, all eyes in on them. So much sass pouring out that too tight dress. And curves... those curves! With legs like pegs, never ending, sending come to bed eyes and opening their thighs as they basically fuck on the dance floor.

C. ⌈I mean, I am a feminist you know, but it goes out the window as I try to attract and interact with you.⌋

Principles I live by, give by, disappear as I try to get your attention by falling into social conventions because apparently I'm not supposed to be intelligent or excellent, everything about me is irrelevant except these tricks we used to get picked up.

But I might as well give up, because you're dancing on the dance floor with a better trickster.

And this is how I know I'm going to be single forever, unable to mingle, sitting in my bed, stuffing my face full of Pringles, because I can't do those tricks.

B. And then some gangly, mangly boy sidles up to me and flattered?

Maybe.

But I look at the dance floor, at those fine specimens of human reproduction coming together moving, feeling, touching, as she wettens and you harden.

And I feel the buzz of that fly buzzing around me and sure he's a nice guy,

But for once I want to be her because I know she's getting laid tonight as I know that she knows that you know stuff!

C. But then Your eyes breakaway from the dance floor, floored by your gaze everyone stands amazed and this is my chance so I try giving *You* a look but something is wrong, I'm holding it for too long, staring, wearing you down, not blinking, freaking you out.

Try again but now I'm just too quick, back and forth as if I've got a twitch, an itch in my eye.

B. And I feel like I am losing my chance because as you dance I know that she knows that you know that this is a wild, crazy adult game of twister, bodies mixing into one another, feeling, exploring, playing with each other.

Her bending like a Barbie and you extending like a sonic screwdriver – driving into her, coming in her.

C. But your eyes continue to wander so one last attempt, I use the toilet as an excuse to sashay past you, slyly catching your eye or seeing them watching my thighs.

I go more frequently just to get You to look at me, the girls start asking questions, coming up with suggestions, one asks if I've got a UTI as I've gone to the toilet five times in the last half hour, offering me tablets to power on through.

ALL. Fuck.

B. So I just stand there and to the gangly guy next to me, I tut aloud but inside I'm aroused.

Beause the thing is I'm not even going to have clumsy, fumbly, bumbly sex with this fly.

Him stuck in his shirt and me unable to undo my skirt with awkward touching and him apologising for his early arrival.

No I'm just going to go home, alone and feel... fucking frustrated.

People think girls like me don't want the "D".

That our hormones aren't developed – But we're thirsty!

C. Then suddenly You move towards the bar, not far from me, this could be my chance;

I think about going up to You and explaining I don't have an infection,

I'm just trying to get your attention, without getting sectioned.

But I don't think that fits into the rule book, so I go rogue as I can't do selfies or Vogue.

B. And this is hard because while You can quench your thirst with human touch the only way I'm controlling and holding in this preoccupation is with pure masturbation.

And it's hard because I want You.

C. And I'm not getting your attention by following these condescensions,

They don't work because I can't pass the test,

I'm a bit of a mess,

I'm too loud, brash,

I make rash decisions, I laugh for too long and I'm sorry but I don't like wearing thongs.

B. But I want you here now.

My eyes have had a taste of you and now I crave you all the time and I want you to be mine and to intertwine our bodies till I don't know where I begin and you stop.

I want to kiss your body, lick your ear and bite your neck.

I want to hear you pant and moan.

I want to feel my legs tense, that rush through my body, the tsunami run up my spine, hands shaking, heart beating, sweat dripping because of you.

But I'm not a massively sexually experienced person.

I can't be flirty or funny or sexy.

C. But I can hold a conversation,

Sure I will swear at every exclamation but I am smart and interesting,

So if you have a thing for a girl who goes from awkward to confident in a flick and a twirl, then maybe I should chat to you and give this thing a whirl.

B. Because I want to tell you that I need you now to take me here, there, anywhere, just to feel you in me.

C. Because while you're cool, calm and collected, you have affected me,

And I'm forgetting what's expected of me,

B. And I don't know what to do

Innocent, naive, call me what you want but I don't know what's right or wrong,

What's forward or not because I'm not a massively sexually experienced person.

I'm just me,

C. And just as I'm about to give up and leave, I catch You taking a second glance, checking me, and for a second I think you might want the chance of getting with me.

B. You walk up to me, and suddenly everything I've dreamed becomes a reality and somehow I lose my vocabulary.

C. The only word I seem able to form is:

(Beat. **A** *talking to boy – "You".)*

A. *(To you.)* Hi?

(Pause.)

B. *(To self.)* Say something.

C. *(To self.)* Anything.

A. *(To you.)* See here's the thing,

C. *(To self.)* What's the thing?

B. *(To self.)* It better be something/

C. *(To self.)* Good/

B. *(To self.)* It better be something/

C. *(To self.)* Anything.

A. *(To you.)* The thing is/

C. *(To self.)* Anything.

B. *(To self.)* The thing has to be something/

C. *(To self.)* Anything. At this point the thing can be anything.

B. *(To self.)* Just say something.

C. *(To self.)* Anything.

A. *(To you.)* I see you.

> *(Beat.)*

B. *(To self.)* What?

C. *(To self.)* Well that was...

B. *(To self.)* Something

C. *(To self)* I guess.

A. *(To you.)* I see you.

I actually see you.

I know everyone sees you but I see you.

I see you more than anyone else sees you. I see you clearer and sharper than they see you. I can see more of you. More of you then they will ever know.

I don't mean in a hippy-dippy, I can see the colour purple oozing out of you kind of way, I just mean... I see you.

(Pause.)

Oh God, I'm not making sense, I mean everyone *can* see you, everyone has eyes, well, except for those people with glass eyes and then there's blind people, but that's not really what I'm talking about, not that I have anything against blind people, this isn't like some "blindism" thing. See what I'm trying to say is everyone sees you but I really see you, you see?

I see you smile.

And I see when you don't.

And I get it.

I really think I get it.

(Pause.)

I'm sorry. I'm assuming things, I just really feel that... I see you. I'm sorry, I apologise this is weird, I get that, this is weird, I'm weird but...

I want to touch you.

Not like that, I mean, maybe like that, one day, in the future. If we wanted and that was a thing and we were, consensually – obviously – I mean – of course, obviously. I'm not a rapist. Who is? I mean people are. But I'm not. Which is what a rapist would probably say. Fuck. Sorry. I don't know what I'm trying to say. Are you hot? I'm sweating. Look at me, I'm sweating. I mean don't look at me because I'm sweating just –

Look at me.

And tell me you don't see me.

(Pause.)

When I look at you everything blends into the background, the world that covers and smothers you fades and I can see you. You become fresh to my eyes, like cold water after a run, my eyes can taste you and nothing has ever tasted like this before.

And I do want to touch you.

But I want to actually feel you.

I want to have that taste run through my fingertips, into my bloodstream and never leave my body. Like I have been kissed by the wind and purified by the rain, you would baptise me and I would fall.

Happily.

Helplessly.

> *(Pause.)*

Look at me.

Do you see me?

I really think you could.

I think I could –

Harder.

Look harder.

Look at me.

> *(Smiles.)*

Hi

ALL. I'm Lucy.

> *(Beat.)*

B & C. FUCK

A. We really hit it off –

C. Ow, Ow, Ow

B. Jesus Christ

A. And one thing lead to another –

C. Left a bit, left a bit

B. No, go right, right

A. And before I knew it –

C. Slower, just ease it –

B. Stop jabbing it –

A. You were my first –

C. It doesn't fit

B. What?

C. It won't go in –

B. Stuff it in

C. How?

B. Shove it up there

C. What if it gets stuck?

A. It was –

B. Push harder

C. What if I don't have the right hole –

B. Push faster

C. What if I don't have any of the holes?

B. Rip the plaster

A. It was –

B & C. FUCK

A. Magical.

       (Beat.)

C. I'm never doing it again.

A. We did it again.

C. No-one is ever doing it again.

A. And again and again.

C. It was horrific –

A. And it got better.

C. Why does no one tell you?

   (Beat.)

B. The first time I bled on the sheets.

C. Did you know in some cultures they hang the bloodied sheets outside the home to prove she was a virgin? It's a patriarchal ownership thing.

B. I was so embarrassed.

C. I wish we claimed that back, not for the patriarchal virgin thing,

B. I didn't know what to do –

C. Just for the openness of the bleeding thing. It just seems more expected, more accepted, more prepared.

B. You saw the sheets and something tweaked inside of me, I inwardly freaked and couldn't speak, I didn't know what to say, I couldn't explain it away,

My mouth was dry as my eyes began to prick,

They burned as I saw you learn of how that was my first turn.

I turned away, needed to find an airway, couldn't breath,

Needed to leave, started to heave.

But you teased the sheets off,

Your hand brushed the stain, and blushed pain rained down on me,

But you didn't flinch, or inch away, you stayed and delayed for a moment,

Considering our fling, you clinged for a second,

Before removing them and improving them with fresh sheets.

Everything, fresh to my eyes.

You looked at me and it shook me as you took me, in your arms and whispered:

ALL. "Sorry."

B. You sat me down and found where the pain pounded. You kissed me slow and soft.

A. And we did it again.

C. And we did it again.

B. And we did it again.

C. And over time,

A. Again and again.

C. It got better.

(Pause.)

B. Twenty five

C. And for a few years we had been having some fun.

B. I was starting to think you were the one.

C. But things had become...

A. Predictable.

B. Not bad –

C. Just a little boring.

B. We were moved in,

C. Out of town

A. Into city,

B. Honeymooning over,

A. And now,

ALL. Reality:

C. Office

B. Eat

A. Sleep

C. Office

B. Eat

A. Sleep

C. Office

B. Eat

A. Sleep

ALL. Repeat.

C. And not a lot of time for, well... anything.

       (Beat.)

B. So I wanted to spice things up a little bit.

C. To experiment a little bit.

B. To explore and learn to adore a little bit more.

A. And so for the first time I went to Ann Summers.

C. I walked past the shop three times before heading in. I knew the security guard recognised me, but he just smiled when I finally made it in. I lingered in the lingerie for ages before I could get up the courage to walk in further. See, the shop is set out in a way that lures me into a false sense of security. As I walk in there is underwear on display, matching pants and bras, and I can almost make myself believe I am in the underwear

section of M&S or something. That's if M&S also sold
suspenders and crotchless pants. So I'm just browsing,
getting a little overwhelmed over the amount of choice;
babydolls, hosiery, chamises, bodices, corsets and that's
not starting on the costumes,

ALL. Hospital hottie, sexy secretary, tuxedo bunny.

A. And then suddenly I am there, down the back, in a little
section of its own and I know I'm not in M&S anymore.
There are penis-things everywhere, cock rings, anal
beads, things for him, for her, for couples. There are
bright pink vibrators, with diamond crustings and
why the fuck would I want a diamond vibrator? What
if one of the cheap diamond sequins comes off inside
me and I can't find it and then I just have to live with
a permanent vajazzle. No way, so I back away. I back
away and into…

ALL. Holy fuck.

B. I back straight into these massive dildos. In all different
shapes and colours and let's be honest, penis' aren't the
most attractive things in the world and if it's not an
actual penis then why would I want it to have all the
veins and wrinkles and stuff. Surely it's just better to
have something that looks nice to put inside me, and
now I'm starting to understand the whole diamond
trend when a woman comes up to me.

C. *(As saleswoman.)* Can I help you?

B. And I freeze, I don't know what to say, I just stare at
her.

C. *(To self.)* Say something.

A. *(To self.)* Anything.

B. *(To saleswoman.)* No thanks I'm just looking.

C. *(As saleswoman.)* Anything in particular?

B. *(To saleswoman.)* No just… well, anything.

(Beat.)

And before I know it, I have this woman picking out couples vibrators for me, showing the lube she personally prefers and holding up lingerie that she thinks will bring out my "eyes". At last I head to the counter, and as it turns out, sex is expensive.

A. I panic buy the lingerie and hand back everything else that collectively makes up half my rent.

B. *(To saleswoman.)* But I promise I'll come back for the rest.

A. And I do, in time.

C. Cut to that evening, and I'm standing over the bath, looking down at myself, considering my vagina more than I ever have before.

B. Does it look okay?

C. How am I supposed to know?

B. Cut, shaven, trimmed,

A. Trimmed, shaven, cut,

B. Styled and restyled.

A. Natural?

B. Bald?

C. Bikini line?

A. Landing strip?

C. I put on my new underwear.

B. I look in the mirror.

C. And I look hot.

B. Like really hot.

C. And don't get me wrong, it's not like I need these things to feel sexy, it's just for the first time I look at myself and looking back at me,

B. I see it,

A. I know what I want.

    (Beat.)

C. That was the first time I actually enjoyed sex.

B. I mean I had always "enjoyed" it but I hadn't realised how much I could enjoy it until I really "enjoyed" it,

C. Until I found that we could enjoy it, properly, together:

    (Beat.)

A. Rewind to *You* getting home early,

C. While I was finishing preparing,

A. Just taking in what I was wearing,

B. As *You* walked in,

C. Talking,

A. And then a momentary panic set in.

B. You saw a glimpse of me, rushing between our bathroom and kitchen.

A. And I started to question.

C. Is this the right decision?

B. What if you laugh when I ask?

A. When I ask for the first time?

C. When I take control?

A. For the first time.

C. When I lead the game.

A. For the first time.

B. But then you see me.

A. And it's like the first time again.

B. You actually see me.

C. And there's a glimmer in your eyes again.

A. A glimmer of relief from what our old, tired game had started to be,

B. To what this new, exciting game could potentially be,

A. And we see each other and now both agree.

C. So you trip and fall in at my feet.

B. And from then I didn't miss a beat. We greet one another, as we have before, your lips pressed against mine, but it's new this time, as you tremble at my touch and I take control.

C. Because alone your dick's not going to make me cum. Sure it's a lot of fun. I like having you inside me, feeling us vibing, both in sync till you start arriving, but I am finding too often, that if you stick to this one trick I am lying there thinking,

ALL. God I hope this is quick.

C. It takes more to make me tick, my orgasm is more complicated that hitting repeat on an in and out streak so listen to me speak, because I'm going to break it down for you.

A. Follow me.

B. I lead you to our bed and inform you of what's ahead, as my legs spread I explain the game as I claim tonight is going to fulfil a different appetite; mine.

ALL. One

C. There is more to me than just a floating vagina, I've got a body that it's attached to, it's the one that attracted you, that you might want to pay a little more attention to.

A. I want you to kiss me.

C. Like a neck or legs or for some people toes is just how it goes. Or lips, maybe tits, nipples that are waiting to be bitten. I want to be kissed and sucked, there is so much more to it than just being touched. Like teeth and nails, it is in the details, because my body is a playground that you got to start exploring or I'm going to start walking away, till I find someone who can handle the game, who can bring more to the table than just their crown jewels, because I'm not going to lose anymore, so maybe you got to choose between folding and rising because I'm not scared to call your bluff.

A. Kiss me.

B. You start on my lips, a gentle clip, to tease me with your taste but you waste no time as the tension starts to climb and you find your way to my neck and in a sec I am buzzing, hair standing on end type of rushing going through me. You move down my body as you get cocky and start to play, your lips stray down my chest, taking a breast at a time as you wind your tongue around.

ALL. Two

C. You got a tongue, use it. You ask me to give you head every time we go to bed, hands on the back of my neck, begging me not to stop, but when I pop the question, just a simple suggestion, a little direction on how to release my tension. A tongue tip against my clit.

A. I want you to use your tongue.

C. You look at me with confusion as the illusion breaks, as you realise I'm also a human looking for a sexual conclusion. As you realise I know what I want and it's more than a quick poke in my hole, as I own my body, I've played with my body and I know what my body wants and it wants a man who knows how to use his tongue, who can make me cum as he wraps it around my legs and the words in my head. [Who can stimulate me both sexually and intellectually with the tongue in his mouth.] I want to be tied up. Tongue tied up as my eyes pop wide as it lies against my body and against my mind, as we both find uses that help me unwind.

A. I want you to use your tongue.

B. Your lips connect with my thighs, opening wide, moving close then swinging to the other side, so close to touching as I clutch harder. You tease and taunt and just as my body's about to explode and implode, needing to scream from frustration and elation; body contracting and impacting in on itself, you touch. Slow at first as the thirst builds, chills run through me as you press onto my senses and you commence, running up and down, round till you found the spot.

ALL. Three

C. And finally, I got these two fingers that I know how to use.

A. I want to touch myself.

C. We have got pretty close over the years and I know what to do, so while you are inside me pumping away, maybe I want to play, want to add another level to our little game. Does that scare you? Is your masculinity threatened at the way I wetten at my own touch? Is it too much to handle, that I want my hands full of me? That your dick might not be all that porn made it out to be, that there may be some other angles that it forgot to see, like me. Like all of me.

A. I want to touch me.

B. My fingertips glide down my body, they slide up my legs and thread themselves into place, tracing as energy starts racing, my body bracing as the chase is on.

C. Is all this too much? Is my empowerment emasculating? My voice degrading, am I too demanding, advancing on commanding?

A. I want you inside me.

B. You look at me and smile. You see me, as you move in, pushing back my legs so I can pull you in deeper, I feel you seep in further, pulsing as I convulse in pleasure. In further, deeper, faster, slower, hitting my buttons as my nails cut into your back. Wrapping my legs, holding on tight as the pleasure reaches new heights. The sensation travelling as vibration through my blood stream, to my fingertips and toes, body in climax from our act, I max out as each cell in my body connects in one electric shockwave running through and the ecstasy flows.

     (Beat.)

Twenty nine.

ALL. SHIT

C. That feeling when the condom splits.

B. Sheer panic passing through.

C. It's almost like I can feel the conception happening.

B. And in that split second I am forty five, living in the suburbs, driving a people carrier and waving little Jimmy off to Uni.

C. My life is over.

B. And of course I'm overreacting and nothing's really happening.

C. But I'm twenty nine

B. The pressure of life passing by.

C. The pressure of girls from school becoming wives.

B. The pressure of everywhere I go there being babies with big, dopey eyes.

    (Beat.)

C. *You* turned to me.

B. Eight years we have been going, *You* said to me:

ALL. "Would it be so bad if we had one of our own?"

A. Time freezes

B. And a question seizes

C. Are we ready to leave our life behind?

B. Are we ready to no longer be free?

A. Are we ready to give up everything we've already achieved?

C. And see, I want it but right now you're looking at me and... we're so happy.

A. And you're looking at me and I wonder if this could be all we need.

B. And you are looking at me...

A. And is it selfish to just want you to be mine for a little longer?

    To want to have all your attention for a little longer?

    To want to have all your love for a little longer?

C. Is it selfish to want to keep my freedom in this moment?

    To want to follow my work in this moment?

    Now that I am enjoying and succeeding in this moment?

B. Is it selfish to wonder if it would be worth it?

    If giving up a life would be worth it?

    If sharing our love would be worth it?

A. Time unfreezes

ALL. *(To you.)* I need a little longer

C. And your hand squeezes mine

B. You look me in the eyes

ALL. "Take your time."

C. Time ticks.

B. Six months slip

A. And the thought sticks, and the stick grows into a want and the want pricks, it picks away.

My eyes start to stray as babies pass by.

And one day I look at you.

I see you.

And it's funny.

Because then I knew.

I can't tell you why or how.

I just knew.

And the love grew.

I loved you.

And I wanted another you

Or me

Another you and me

I wanted to make something out of this perfect entity.

I wanted to make a person out of the person I loved.

B. I take your hand.

A. *(To you.)* Look at me.

C. I squeeze.

B. You see me.

A. *(To you.)* Let's make us three.

C. Time ticks

B. One month slips

A. I was addicted.

I was addicted to how you held me, to how your tongue danced down my body.

I was addicted to how you kissed open my thighs.

I was addicted to how you took me in your mouth first.

I was addicted to how you played with me.

I was addicted to how you felt in me.

C. Time ticks

B. Three months slip

A. I was addicted.

I was addicted to trying.

I was addicted to making you cum.

I was addicted to making schedules and routines and taking tests.

C. Time ticks

B. Six months slip

A. I was addicted.

I was addicted to getting it done.

I was addicted to having you inside me for a few seconds at a time, to finding the quickest way, to pushing through the warm up and putting you in, to move past the tightness and the jarring and to just conceive.

C. Time ticks

B. Nine months slip

A. I was addicted.

And I was sick of you. Sick of you taking your time, and wasting mine. I was sick of you finding new ways to play. I was sick of you kissing me and wanting me and enjoying me. I was sick of you not just doing your job.

ALL. Don't touch me, just fuck me.

A. I was addicted.

C. Time ticks

B. Eleven months slip

A. I was addicted.

And I hated myself. I didn't know why I couldn't. Why everything I was told I should just wouldn't. I didn't know what was wrong with me. Why part of you didn't want to join with me.

Why someone didn't want to grow in me.

But I was addicted.

C. Time ticks

B. And it took thirteen months and eleven days to slip.

C. For something to click.

A. Five

B. Four

C. Three

A. Two

B. One

ALL. Positive.

B. At last I could breathe.

C. I felt myself start to heave.

B. I could hardly believe.

A. We finally conceived. And I was –

B. / Ecstatic

C. Terrified

A. We were free from everything, all the/

B. Tests and temperature taking

C. The waiting and wanting

B. The restriction from sex

C. And then the friction from sex.

B. The fear.

C. The blame.

B. And the unrelenting shame.

A. Gone. And renewed with...

B. Indescribable joy. A love pounding inside of me joy. A want to scream from the rooftops joy. A need to cry and laugh from this overpowering joy.

C. And fear. A new fear. A rewind time fear. A nothing is ever going to be the same fear. A can I do this fear?

B. What we had wanted for so long,

C. And then it's real.

   I mean I had to check it was real

   I couldn't believe it was real

   After all the negatives

   I couldn't believe the positive

   I peed constantly

   On stick after stick

   On our stock pile of pregnancy tests

I peed on them all

And then I told *You*

It was real.

You took me and shook your head,

ALL. "Don't joke with me"

B. I showed you the tests

Your eyes instantly filled and spilled over, you held me, you laughed, you cried

You couldn't believe it was real, so we went out and bought a whole new set of pregnancy tests

And yeah pregnancy is expensive

But we bought them all

And I had never been so delighted to pee

And you had never been so delighted to watch me pee

As I sat on the toilet

And you held my hand

As we both grinned uncontrollably

And I peed until I could pee no more

Until there were more positives than negatives.

And it was real.

We were doing this.

     (Pause.)

A. Weeks started to pass and I felt them settle. ⌈I know they were nothing more than a couple of cells coming together but it was as if I could feel them building their home, getting comfortable for the next nine months. And as they made their nest in me, I settled too.⌉ I relaxed into carrying them, the fear sunk a little as we started to get to know each other.

B. And physically nothing changes outside but inside my body is churning and Mum knows the second she sees me, I try to deny out of convention but she sees right through me. She whispers congratulations in my ear and it starts to become reality. And then –

C. Time ticks.

B. Twelve weeks slip.

C. I wake to a shooting pain in my back.

I curl into the cramp, and clutch round my stomach as I try to cling to it.

I feel something compressing around me, twisting my insides tight as the pain deepens.

I feel a warmth between my legs and I can't move, but I know.

⌠ So I lay in my blood before you wake.

I want you to stay asleep so I can keep them for a little longer. ⌡

I thought if I didn't move, they would still be a part of me.

That my body could be all they needed.

They needed me.

So I stay still.

I feel them leave me.

I press my legs shut.

I try to hold on.

I try to hold them in.

I don't give up.

They are mine.

And I don't know why my body stopped loving them.

Because I never did.

>   *(Beat.)*

And I don't move, for fear of waking you.

I don't want you to break this moment.

I don't want you to make me leave them.

I don't want to look you in the eye.

>   *(Beat.)*

I don't want you to see the stained sheets.

I don't want you to see how I have failed.

>   *(Beat.)*

But then you wake –

ALL. I'm fine.

C. You start to –

ALL. Please give me more time.

>   *(Beat.)*

C. You hold me.

The sensation is numbing.

Like a physical silence piercing through my body.

Tearing up and in and pulling me out.

It happened so fast, yet everything was slow.

It's over in seconds but it never stopped.

>   *(Beat.)*

You rushed me there.

And you did everything right.

As I sat there bleeding.

Then they told us there.

That our baby was gone.

And you did everything right.

Then they told us there.

That they needed to make it stop.

To make the bleeding stop.

So they opened me with pliers where you used to use your fingers.

They took a knife to me where you used to take a tongue.

You did everything right.

As they scraped away the walls of my insides which should have been looking after something warm and alive.

You did everything right.

As they tried to stop me bleeding from the gaping gap where my child should have been born.

B. And then

A. You took me home.

B. You held me tight

A. You laid me down

B. You kissed me,

A. Goodnight.

B. And as I laid in those sheets something tweaked inside of me, I inwardly freaked but I couldn't speak,

I didn't know what to say about how you had just
hidden it all away.

My mouth was dry but my eyes began to prick,

They burned as I saw, as I learned that you had teased
those sheets off.

My sheets off. Their sheets were gone.

Your hand would have brushed the stains and pain
rained down on me.

Did you flinch?

Or inch away?

Did you stay or delay for a moment?

Did you cling for a second?

Did you consider anything before removing them and
improving them with fresh sheets?

Everything, fresh to my eyes, against my skin, it buried
in and pinned me in a strangers sheets.

And I know you were just trying to do what's right and
you had done everything right but you had no right.

They were my sheets.

My sheets to clean.

My sheets to keep.

My sheets to prove it was something I went through.

My sheets to hang in the streets to show the world that
I had a baby too.

> *(Beat.)*

You just looked at me and it shook me as you took me
by my arms and sat me down and tried but couldn't
find where the pain pounded.

(Beat.)

C. Time ticks

A. Thirty one slips

C. Kisses miss and words drift.

A. Nothing fills the ache in the abyss.

C. Something between us

B. Gone

A. Changed

C. Something doesn't quite feel the same.

B. You try to fix, but nothing fits

A. "Look at me"

C. You beg me

B. But I can't

A. I can't see you and I can't see me anymore, we're just blurry

C. So I try to avoid you

B. To avoid us

A. And reality hits

C. Office

B. Eat

A. Sleep

C. Office

B. Eat

A. Sleep

C. Office

B. Eat

A. Sleep

ALL. Repeat.

C. And I make sure there isn't a lot of time for, well... anything else.

B. We've tried some things, but actually doing everything. Actually being together again, it isn't really a thing yet.

A. So I stay late at work

C. I work constantly

B. Just to be in a place where nothing's changed

A. No-one knew so no-one asks

B. No-one knows that I'm mummy. And that you're a daddy. And that I was pregnant but I'm without a baby.

C. And then I get home and You try so hard:

A. "Do you blame me?"

B. You ask me

A. And you break my heart.

C. Because rationally I know you did everything right/

B. Everyone did everything right/

A. The nurses/

C. The doctors/

B. My mother/

A. You/

B. But that doesn't stop me being angry/

C. It still hurts me.

A. And then you look at me... "I'm hurting too."

B. You tell me

A. "I'm grieving too"

C. You tell me

A. "But I'm not just grieving our baby"

C. You tell me

A. "I'm grieving you."

C. You tell me

A. "I've lost you"

C. I still love you

B. I tell you

C. And you cry

A. "Can we at least try?"

B. You ask me

C. And I see you.

A. "How about a date?"

B. Okay

A. "Why don't we play our game?"

C. Okay I say

A. Date one:

B. You walk in, we try talking, we trip and end up falling, stumbling over sentences and stalling.

A. Date two:

C. I use the toilet as an excuse to break away, slyly catching your eye and seeing you see right through me knowing the real reason why.

A. Date three:

B. We try holding a look but something is wrong.

A. Date four:

C. You find me in bed, unable to mingle, mindlessly stuffing my face full of Pringles and a smile starts to tingle.

B. You look at me as I used to be, sitting in sheets invisibly stained by our history. Sheets that make up everything we used to be, sheets that hold everything we could be.

C. And a world starts to unpeel, the idea that sharing something stupid like eating crisps in our sheets might finally let us heal.

A. We sit

C. And eat

B. We watch

A. Mindlessly

C. We talk

B. Occasionally

A. We look

C. With uncertainty

B. You touch

A. Hesitantly

C. I flinch

B. Automatically

A. You wait

C. Accordingly

B. Then try again

A. Systematically

C. I'm still

B. Reassuringly

A. You continue

C. Hopefully

B. I'm still

A. Promisingly

C. You kiss

B. For the first time.

C. But your lips shake as they touch mine.

B. I taste your tears as they fall on my tongue.

C. Your nose begins to run, everything mixes together as you kiss me.

B. You press hard against me, sobbing into me.

C. You hold me until it hurts.

B. Your hands start to move

C. Trembling as they touch me

A. I whisper –

B. Then they go to my shirt.

C. Your lips go to my neck

B. You whisper –

ALL. "Please."

B. You look at me

C. And I see you

A. I actually see you

C. I see what you need

B. And I love you

A. And I so want to be able to be what you need

C. So...

(*Beat.*)

A. It's funny,

Not funny, funny,

Like laughing funny,

Just funny like interesting funny,

Or unbelievable funny,

Why funny,

The frustrating kind of funny

Because I just laid there

And I was dry – really really... like sandpaper kind of dry.

I wasn't...

Not even discharge wet.

It was like,

You know when you go to the dentist and there's so much saliva in your mouth that it's getting in the way and so they get this suction machine, it's this tube that goes in your mouth and sucks it dry.

So dry that you're trying to gag up some sort of spit or something just to dampen even a little bit because it is so horrible being that dry.

Well it was like that.

It was as if they had got one of those tubes, stuck it down there and sucked every last drip out of me.

It was that kind of dry.

It was skin on skin,

Creating a burning.

I actually thought it was on the fire at one point.

And I know that sounds stupid,

But afterwards I couldn't put my legs together,

Could barely walk because of…

So I got loads of sudocrem, for rashes and stuff and just kind of bathed my… in it.

But it stung like… like a million bee's had swarmed down on me.

I ran into the bath and just sat there crying.

Watching it bleed into the water.

That was the first time I cried.

Funny isn't it?

During everything that happened I never cried.

You were the only one who cried.

And it's funny, because I just knew that when you were on me, in me, and I looked in your eyes as you cried and I knew…

You needed this.

I always knew you needed this.

Which is funny,

Sad funny because I can't tell you why or how,

I just knew,

Within myself.

My gut saw that look,

You needed this.

And I just think, I hope you got what you needed because then at least the pain of the dryness would have been worth it.

Like looking in your eyes and knowing you needed this more than I could understand, that maybe we needed this more than I could understand

Because I didn't understand

I just knew,

I had to push through.

(*Beat.*)

And do you know what the funniest thing is?

Now, I don't even look at it or touch it.

I'm just sitting in the bath avoiding it.

It's funny because with…

They're so tucked away that if I try hard enough I can almost forget about it.

Because now, it's like after everything, I look at it and I really don't know it.

It's funny because I'm sitting in the bath, looking down at it and it's like it's gone back to just being a funny thing.

And an old thought comes back in, as I look at it, I think;

ALL. What is that funny thing?

(*Beat.*)

A. Only this time a whisper starts answering and suddenly I'm thinking about barbies bashing together, about sonic screwdrivers coming in her, about massive dildos covered in wrinkles. I'm thinking about kisses, about first times and last times, I am thinking about sheets. I am thinking about them, about the tests and the pain and I'm thinking about You.

But mostly I'm thinking about what happens if I just sit here. If I just sit here and you just sit there. If I sit here in the bath and you look at me. You look at me sitting here.

C. Cramped in

A. Sitting here

B. Wet

(repeated opening)

C. Cramped in

A. Sitting here

C. Looking at me

A. Sitting here

B. Too late

C. Is it too late?

A. To sit here

B. And start

C. Again?

A. I want them

B. Their millions of nerves

C. Their heartbeat

B. Something with a heartbeat inside of me

A. I want

C. A beat

A. I want

B. Them

C. To sit here

B. With me

A. And

B. It hurts

C. It's suffocating

B. It's isolating

C. But it's funny

A. I could

C. Laugh

A. Because it's funny

B. Me

A. Sitting here

B. You

C. Looking at me

A. Sitting here

C. Look

B. At

A. Me

B. I want

C. You

B. Let me help

C. You heal

A. My body can heal

C. Heal my body

B. We can heal as I

C. Touch and

A. Trace

B. Trace my skin

C. Connecting

B. Everything

A. Connecting every inch

C. Inch closer

B. And now you

C. Look

B. At

A. Me

C. As I

A. Sit here

B. Sparkling

A. Again

B. I'm looking like

C. I want

A. My

B. I want

A. Me

C. I want

A. No?

B. Maybe

C. Yes

A. I want to

B. Try

C. To pump life

B. To consume

C. To play

A. To sit here

B. And look at me

C. I want

B. Again

A. To sit here

C. And start again

A. To try

B. A touch

A. To try

C. Touching

A. Me

B. I want to

A. Sit here

C. Cramped in

B. Wet

A. I want to sit here

C. And

B. Understand

A. I want you

B. I want them

C. I want me

A. So I

B. Touch

A. And I start

ALL. Again.

ABOUT THE AUTHOR

Sarah Richardson is an award-winning playwright, actor and spoken word poet. Originally from London, Sarah trained at The Gaiety School of Acting in Dublin.

As a poet Sarah has performed across the UK and Ireland, on tour and at poetry events and festivals including Electric Picnic and Knockanstockan. Awards received include Inter-Varsity Slam Champion 2018 and Leinster Poetry Slam Champion 2018.

GirlPlay is Sarah's debut play. Originally staged at Dublin Fringe 2019, *GirlPlay* was adapted into an audio play in 2020 and went on to have an international digital tour, winning Best Digital Experience at Stockholm Fringe Festival. *GirlPlay* was restaged at Camden People's Theatre in October 2021, supported by Culture Ireland and Arts Council England and is now heading to Edinburgh Fringe 2022 as a supported company with theSpaceUK.

Sarah has been the recipient of the Axis Assemble Associate Artist programme (2020) and FringeLab Artist programme (2020) for the development of her one woman show, Sun Bear. She was also selected to be a part of NSDF Lab 2021/2, where she created a piece of teen theatre, A Ton of Feathers, that was presented at the NSDF festival 2022.

Lightning Source UK Ltd.
Milton Keynes UK
UKHW020639310722
406617UK00005B/672